US SPECIAL FORCES

GREEN BERETS

By Drew Nelson

Gareth Stevens
Publishing

Please visit our website, www.garethstevens.com. For a free color catalog of all our high-quality books, call toll free 1-800-542-2595 or fax 1-877-542-2596.

Library of Congress Cataloging-in-Publication Data

Nelson, Drew.
Green Berets / Drew Nelson.
    p. cm. — (US special forces)
Includes bibliographical references and index.
ISBN 978-1-4339-6559-3 (pbk.)
ISBN 978-1-4339-6560-9 (6-pack)
ISBN 978-1-4339-6557-9 (library binding)
1. United States. Army. Special Forces—Juvenile literature. I. Title.
UA34.S64N49 2012
356'.167—dc23

2011031673

First Edition

Published in 2012 by
Gareth Stevens Publishing
111 East 14th Street, Suite 349
New York, NY 10003

Copyright © 2012 Gareth Stevens Publishing

Designer: Michael J. Flynn
Editor: Kristen Rajczak

Photo credits: Cover, p. 1 MILpictures by Tom Weber/The Image Bank/Getty Images; photos courtesy of US Army: pp. 4–5 by Angelo Jasper, 8, 18–19 by USACE, 20, 21 by Gilian M. Albro, 22–23 by Spc. Amanda McBride, 4th IBCT Public Affairs, 23 by Lance Cpl. Cristina Noeila Gil, 24 by Air Force 2nd Lt. Victoria Brayton, 25 by Pfc. Kim, Tae Hoon, 26–27 by Spc. Elisabet Freeburg, 29 by Mr. Walter Sokalski; pp. 6–7 Bernard Hoffman/ Time & Life Pictures/Getty Images; p. 9 Ralph Crane/Time & Life Pictures/Getty Images; p. 11 Ralph Morse/ Time & Life Pictures/Getty Images; pp. 12–13 John Dominis/Time & Life Pictures/Getty Images; p. 14 Bloomberg/ Getty Images; p. 15 Shutterstock.com; pp. 16–17 Joe Raedle/Getty Images.

Printed in the United States of America

CPSIA compliance information: Batch #CW12GS: For further information contact Gareth Stevens, New York, New York at 1-800-542-2595.

CONTENTS

Words in the glossary appear in **bold** type the first time they are used in the text.

WHO ARE THE GREEN BERETS?

The US Army Special Forces have a nickname: the Green Berets. The name comes from the green hats that are an official part of their uniforms. They're specially trained soldiers who work in small groups to carry out secret **missions** too difficult for regular soldiers. They fight and work all over the world, during both times of war and times of peace.

These Special Forces soldiers wear green berets as part of their uniform.

The job of the Green Berets is to keep Americans safe. They carry out many different kinds of missions to make sure that happens. They fight enemies, but they also do other secret activities and spread goodwill to other nations.

The Green Beret

A beret is a small, round hat usually thought of as French. As early as 1953, green berets were used as unofficial headgear for Special Forces soldiers when they were in the field. During the early 1960s, the Department of the Army made it the official headgear of the US Army Special Forces.

BEFORE THE GREEN BERETS

There were many other kinds of Special Forces in the army before the Green Berets. During World War II, the army created the Office of Strategic Services (OSS) to collect secret information about the enemy. They traveled into enemy territory to help local resistance groups in their secret stuggle against the enemy.

In 1942, a group of Canadian and American soldiers in Montana formed the First Special Service Force. They were trained in mountain climbing and in air and water operations. They fought in the mountains of Italy and in the waters around southern France before being shut down in December 1944.

Other Early Army Special Forces

The Army Rangers: These World War II soldiers fought in small groups and were trained to work in many challenging **environments**.

Merrill's Marauders: This 3,000-man force fought in China and India during World War II. They specialized in traveling long distances quickly to attack enemy forces.

Merrill's Marauders cross a river in Burma during World War II.

HISTORY OF THE GREEN BERETS

The first Special Forces group was established in May 1952 at Fort Bragg, North Carolina, by the Special Operations Division of the **Psychological Warfare** Center. First, the Army Rangers, who had been fighting in the **Korean War**, were shut down. Then, the army gave the new 10th Special Forces Group 2,300 spots to fill with specially trained soldiers—the first Green Berets.

Colonel Aaron Bank was the group's first commander. He believed the United States needed a group ready for "unconventional warfare." This term may mean different things to different people. However, it usually involves fighting that's different from standard battles and commonly includes secret activities in enemy territory.

Today's Green Berets can trace their roots to these men—the First Special Service Force.

The First Green Berets

The 10th Special Forces Group only had 10 members when it first formed. This included Colonel Aaron Bank, one other officer, and eight **enlisted** soldiers. Within a few months, however, soldiers started training for the group by the hundreds, quickly making the team a stronger unit.

Former OSS officers, ex-Rangers, and other experienced troops were part of the first group of Green Berets, shown here training for battle.

THE GREEN BERETS IN KOREA

By the end of 1952, the Green Berets had already grown into an important part of the US Army. A few members of the 10th Special Forces Group became some of the first Army Special Forces troops to be **deployed** behind enemy lines. They were placed on islands along the North Korean coast and trained local fighters, called "Donkeys" or "Wolfpacks," to raid enemy camps and rescue downed airmen.

Guided by these Special Forces, the "Wolfpack" fighters eventually grew to more than 22,000 men. They reported killing or capturing 69,000 North Korean enemies.

The Special Forces ODA

By 1958, the basic Green Beret team for each mission had become a 12-soldier unit known as an Operations Detachment Alpha, or ODA. A detachment is a small military group. ODAs included two officers, two operations and **intelligence** sergeants, two weapons sergeants, two communications sergeants, two medics, and two engineers.

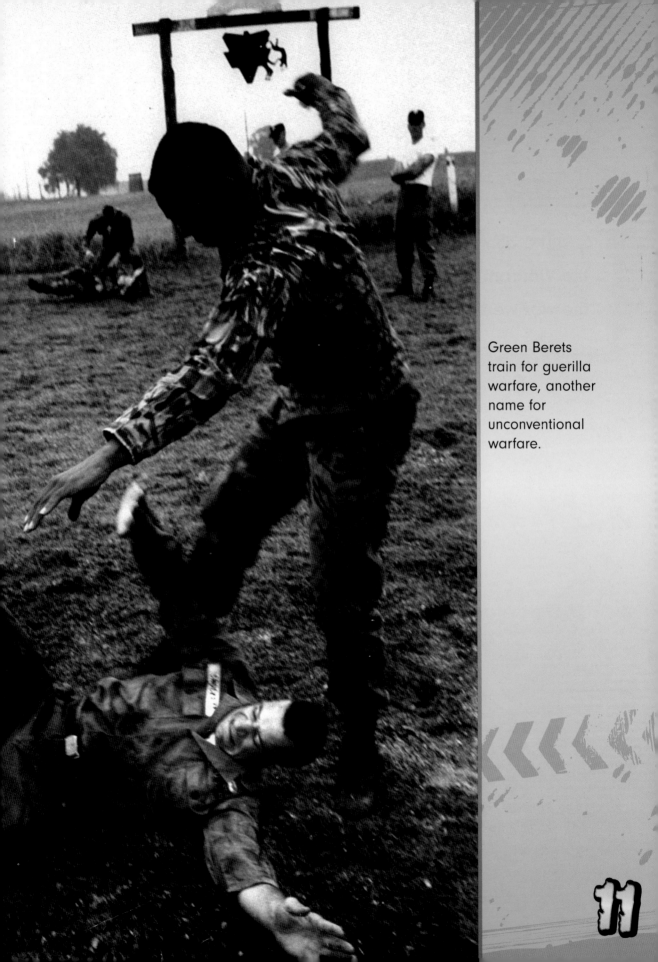

Green Berets train for guerilla warfare, another name for unconventional warfare.

THE GREEN BERETS IN VIETNAM

The US Army Special Forces were very important throughout the **Vietnam War**. In fact, the first and last soldiers killed during the war were both Green Berets.

This US Army sergeant is training Vietnamese troops for battle in 1961.

The Green Berets were first deployed to South Vietnam in June 1957 to train local fighters in **counterinsurgency**. More Green Berets arrived during the late 1950s and early 1960s. They trained Vietnamese tribes to become fighting forces. They also built schools and hospitals, and dug canals to help the people of South Vietnam. By the time the Green Berets left in 1972, their bravery had been recognized by many honors, including 17 Medals of Honor.

The Son Tay Raid

In 1970, the Green Berets planned a secret mission to break into a Vietnamese prison camp to free US soldiers. They spent months planning every part of the attack and completed the raid perfectly in only 27 minutes. Unfortunately, the US prisoners had been moved, and the camp was empty.

THE GREEN BERETS IN POPULAR CULTURE

The top-secret missions and difficult training of the US Army Special Forces have always interested the American people. The Green Berets have made many appearances in music and movies and even as toys.

Sylvester Stallone stars in *Rambo*.

In 1966, former Special Forces Staff Sergeant Barry Sadler had a hit in the United States with the song "Ballad of the Green Berets." It was released on an album of songs about being a soldier during the Vietnam War. Many G.I. Joe action figures were made in the late 1960s to look like Green Berets, too. A popular film character of the 1980s, John Rambo, was supposed to be a former US Army Special Forces soldier.

The Congressional Medal of Honor

The Congressional Medal of Honor is the highest award the United States gives for bravery. Since its creation in 1861, the president has only given out about 3,450 medals. In 2010, Staff Sergeant Robert Miller, a Green Beret, was awarded the Medal of Honor after he died serving in Afghanistan.

TYPES OF MISSIONS

There are five main kinds of missions that the Green Berets carry out. They are direct action, special reconnaissance, counterterrorism, foreign internal defense, and unconventional warfare.

US Army Special Forces often work with local soldiers, such as the Iraqi commando on the left.

In direct action, Green Berets quickly attack enemy targets. In special reconnaissance, they sneak into enemy locations to gather intelligence. In counterterrorism, Green Berets follow the actions of **terrorist** groups and act directly against them to prevent terrorist attacks. In foreign internal defense, they train and help soldiers in other countries respond to threats from common enemies. In unconventional warfare, Green Berets use their training to fight with forces in enemy-held territory.

Equipment for Every Mission

The Green Berets must be prepared for any type of mission. To do this, they have a wide variety of equipment. This includes parachutes for jumping out of planes, night-vision goggles for nighttime missions, kayaks, and axes and harnesses for mountain climbing.

17

LOCATIONS OF THE GREEN BERET TEAMS

There are five different Army Special Forces Teams based at duty stations around the country. The 1st Special Forces Group is at Fort Lewis in Washington State. The 3rd and 7th Special Forces Groups are both located at Fort Bragg in North Carolina, the original training site of the Green Berets. The 5th Special Forces Group is located at Fort Campbell in Kentucky, and the 10th Special Forces Group is at Fort Carson in Colorado.

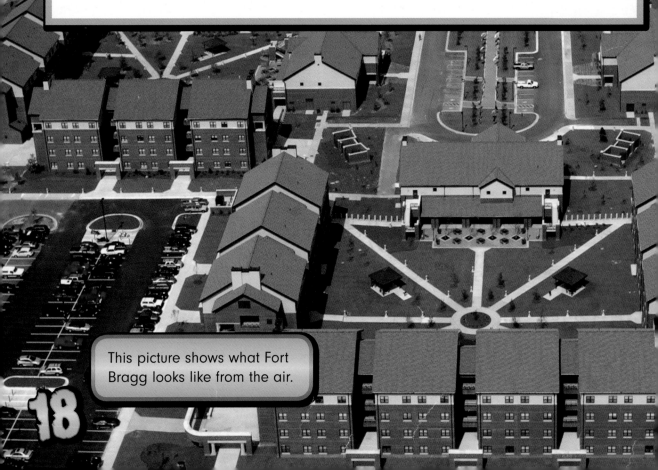

This picture shows what Fort Bragg looks like from the air.

Green Berets are also deployed to Okinawa, Japan; Puerto Rico; and Stuttgart, Germany, so they can reach destinations faster if an emergency occurs in a different part of the world.

Fort Bragg, the Home of the Green Berets

Fort Bragg, located near Fayetteville, North Carolina, is the home of the US Army Special Forces training school. It was established in 1918, and after the Psychological Warfare Center was opened there in 1952, it became the center for the Green Berets' and the army's unconventional warfare training.

TRAINING TO BE A GREEN BERET

The training to be a Green Beret is one of the toughest US Army programs. It starts with the same basic training every soldier must complete. Then, soldiers must go to a 30-day Special Operations Preparation Course at Fort Bragg to prepare for the physical tests in the rest of their training. But even after this course, a soldier still may not qualify to become a Green Beret.

After the preparation course, soldiers take part in the Special Forces Assessment and Selection (SFAS) at Camp Mackall, North Carolina. This is a 24-day program that tests the soldiers' mental and physical endurance with marches, runs, **obstacle courses**, and team exercises.

Soldiers take on the obstacle course during SFAS.

The SFAS

The Special Forces Assessment and Selection camp is held four times a year, with around 300 soldiers attempting the program each time. During the course, the candidates are kept awake for a long time and put under mental and physical pressure. By the second week, more than half the candidates have either quit the program or been removed by instructors.

Soldiers work together to carry heavy boxes during a 15-mile (24 km) hike at Camp Mackall.

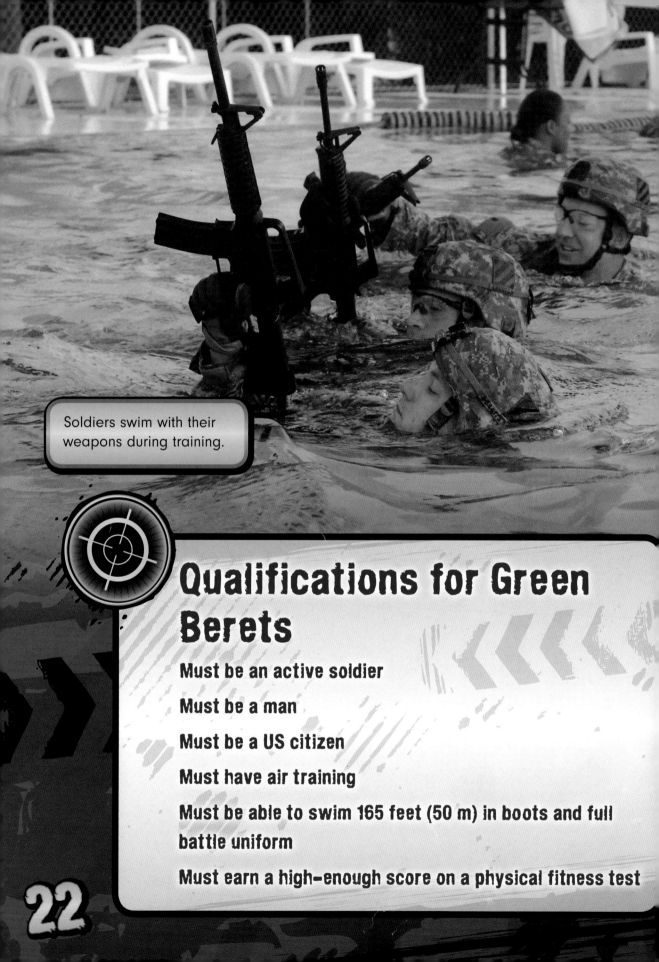

Soldiers swim with their weapons during training.

Qualifications for Green Berets

Must be an active soldier

Must be a man

Must be a US citizen

Must have air training

Must be able to swim 165 feet (50 m) in boots and full battle uniform

Must earn a high-enough score on a physical fitness test

The candidates who make it through the SFAS then move on to the Special Forces Qualification Course. This five-step program prepares soldiers to become Green Berets.

First, soldiers work on individual skills, such as land **navigation** and small-unit **tactics**. Next, they complete Military Occupation Specialty training, in which each soldier learns different skills based on his background and interests.

The next step is collective training, where soldiers learn to work in ODA groups. After this, all candidates take part in language training, where they learn at least one other language. The final part is a Survival, Evasion, Resistance, and Escape (SERE) course.

Soldiers have to be ready for anything. These men are eating grub worms in case they have to find food in the wild.

CITIZENS OF THE WORLD

During peacetime, the main mission of the Green Berets is foreign internal defense. They help people all over the world. The Green Berets work with many nations' military and police forces on various skills, human rights issues, and **humanitarian** projects.

Members of the US Army Special Operations Command help a group of children in Haiti.

In order to do this, most Green Berets go through Live Environment Training. Here, they receive training that puts them completely into a new society. In addition to learning to speak the country's language, Green Berets learn the customs and traditions of that country so they can live like a citizen. With this training, they can better serve the people of these nations.

This group of soldiers is learning about Korean customs and communication.

The Special Forces Motto

The motto of the Green Berets is *De Oppresso Liber*. This is Latin for "To Free the Oppressed." Green Berets are trained to help people in need, whether they're US citizens or not.

MODERN MISSIONS AND THE FUTURE

Since the terrorist attacks on the United States in 2001, the US Army Special Forces have played a big part in US military actions.

The US military started Operation Enduring Freedom in Afghanistan to fight the terrorists responsible for the attacks. The 5th Special Forces Group joined a group known as Task Force Dagger and helped control operations there. Starting in October 2001, the Green Berets also worked with local tribes to fight terrorists and find those who had gone into hiding. In addition, the 3rd and 7th Special Forces Groups helped train and fight with the Afghan army and police forces.

Green Berets by Air

The Green Berets are transported into enemy territory by the 160th Special Operations Aviation Regiment (SOAR), also known as the Nightstalkers. They operate many different kinds of helicopters, including Blackhawks for attacks, smaller Little Birds for secret missions, and Chinooks for long-distance travel.

These M-ATVs help US soldiers get around in the Afghan desert.

In March 2003, the United States started Operation Iraqi Freedom to overthrow the government of Iraq. The 5th Green Beret group was there soon after to prevent the Iraqis from firing long-range bombs. The 10th group operated Task Force Viking to train, arm, and fight with local military and citizens to secure the country's borders.

The Green Berets will continue to carry out special missions, both fighting as soldiers and helping to support other friendly nations. Above all else, their job is and always will be to operate all over the world to make sure that Americans are safe.

Bronze Bruce

In the US Army's Special Command Memorial Plaza at Fort Bragg, there's a Special Warfare Memorial statue known as "Bronze Bruce." Built in 1969, it was the first Vietnam War memorial in the United States. "Bronze Bruce" is 22 feet (6.7 m) tall, and its base contains a Special Forces uniform and a green beret.

"Bronze Bruce" honors the brave Green Berets.

GREEN BERET
SYMBOL OF EXCELLENCE — BADGE OF COURAGE
MARK OF DISTINCTION — SIGN OF THE BEST OF
FREEDOM — PRESIDENT JOHN F KENNEDY

GLOSSARY

counterinsurgency: a military activity of defense against a group trying to overthrow a government

deploy: to move troops into a position of readiness

enlisted: members of the military who rank below commissioned officers

environment: surroundings

equipment: tools, clothing, and other items needed for a job

humanitarian: having to do with working for the health and safety of other people

intelligence: secret information about enemies

Korean War: a conflict between North and South Korea that began in 1950 and ended in 1953

mission: a task or job a group must perform

navigation: the science of plotting and following a path from one place to another

obstacle course: a training area in which objects such as fences and ditches have to be climbed or crossed over

psychological warfare: assaults directed toward or meant to affect the mind

tactics: a method for accomplishing a military goal

terrorist: someone who uses violence and fear to challenge an authority

Vietnam War: a conflict starting in 1957 and ending in 1975 between South Vietnam and North Vietnam in which the United States joined with South Vietnam

FOR MORE INFORMATION

Books

Besel, Jennifer M. *The Green Berets.* Mankato, MN: Capstone Press, 2011.

Nobleman, Marc Tyler. *Green Berets in Action.* New York, NY: Bearport Publishing, 2008.

Sutherland, Adam. *Special Forces.* Minneapolis, MN: Lerner Publications, 2012.

Websites

U.S. Army
www.goarmy.com/special-forces.html
Learn more about how to become a Green Beret.

U.S. Army Special Operations Command
www.soc.mil
Read more about the US Army Special Forces on their official website.

Publisher's note to educators and parents: Our editors have carefully reviewed these websites to ensure that they are suitable for students. Many websites change frequently, however, and we cannot guarantee that a site's future contents will continue to meet our high standards of quality and educational value. Be advised that students should be closely supervised whenever they access the Internet.

INDEX